TOM D

MW00988492

ADVANCED RETRIEVER TRAINING

The Complete Guide to Developing Your Hunting Dog

Copyright ©2013 Tom Dokken

All rights reserved. No portion of this publication may be reproduced or transmitted in any form or by any means, electronic or mechanical, including photocopy, recording, or any information storage and retrieval system, without permission in writing from the publisher, except by a reviewer who may quote brief passages in a critical article or review to be printed in a magazine or newspaper, or electronically transmitted on radio, television, or the Internet.

Published by

Krause Publications, a division of F+W Media, Inc.
700 East State Street • Iola, WI 54990-0001
715-445-2214 • 888-457-2873
www.krausebooks.com

To order books or other products call toll-free 1-800-258-0929
or visit us online at www.krausebooks.com

ISBN-13: 978-1-4402-3453-8
ISBN-10: 1-4402-3453-1

Designed by Tom Nelsen
With Kyle Wintersteen
Edited by Brian Lovett
Cover & Book Photography by Lee Kjos

Printed in China

Dedication

To my family — Mom, Dad, Jule, Scotty, Joanne and Ron. Thanks for making this possible. And special thanks to Sam, for introducing me to my best friend, hunting and fishing partner, and No. 1 supporter — my wife, Tina.

About the Author

Tom Dokken has more than 40 years of experience turning retrievers into successful field-trial competitors, hunt-test participants, waterfowling companions and upland bird finders. His business, Dokken's Oak Ridge Kennels in Northfield, Minn., is one of the largest all-breed hunting dog training facilities in the United States. Tom is also well-known as the creator of the popular Dokken's Deadfowl Trainer training dummy, which he designed to help teach dogs the proper hold on game birds. Tom and his wife, Tina, make their home in Northfield.

Contents

Acknowledgments

This book is the culmination of 40 years of dog training, including thousands of hours in the field, and a lot of time on the road conducting seminars. The training program described is the result of decades of painstaking research and trial and error, of which I've loved every minute.

However, it wouldn't have been possible without all the help I've received from people in the field along the way. These kind folks are too numerous to mention, but they know who they are. Thank you.

I'd also like to thank my wife for her love and support. Most important, Tina, thank you for all the good times spent together in the field with our own personal dogs. I cannot adequately express how much I've enjoyed it.

Another worthy acknowledgement goes to photographer Lee Kjos, whose work will amaze you as you leaf through these pages. Lee is the best in the business and a close personal friend. It is truly my honor that he's lent his talents to this book. Thank you, Lee, for making it truly something spectacular.

Introduction

There are hunters who consider a retriever to be "polished" if he sits, stays, retrieves marked singles and won't run off. Terrific. If such hunters are able to enjoy their dogs without advancing beyond basic training techniques, more power to them. However, retrievers of every breed have so much more potential to offer. It's in their genes, having been bred into them for hundreds of years. To unlock that magic requires dedication, knowledge and a passion on the part of the trainer for bringing out the very best in his animals.

This book is about reaching that next level with your retriever. It was written with the assumption that you've already read my first book, *Tom Dokken's Retriever Training: The Complete Guide to Developing Your Hunting Dog*, and that your dog is ready for extremely high-level training. By the time you're done reading, you'll know much of what it took me 40 years to discover about training retrievers.

The pages are laid out in a format that's intended to be easy to follow. Each chapter charts the course of a particular topic and will help you to progress in small, incremental steps toward the ultimate in hunting dog training — the advanced retriever. Only a small percentage of dogs ever reach the level of training you're about to embark upon, and there's a reason for that: the time and commitment it requires. However, when you've finished all the chapters in this book, your dog will be able to do things you never thought possible, including multiple marked retrieves, honoring another dog's work and, the hallmarks of a polished retriever, blind retrieves over land and water.

Keep in mind that to reach that point, it's necessary that you've maintained the basic skills discussed in book No. 1. If this isn't the case (be honest with yourself), go back, and revisit them. You'll save yourself and your dog a lot of frustration.

A year or two from now, I hope you can look back at where your dog started and be proud of what the two of you have accomplished. And ultimately, someday when you're in a duck blind or the uplands, I hope you can say with honesty that you helped your dog reach his fullest potential. To do so is admirable.

Tom Dokken,
March 2013

–1–

EQUIPMENT FOR THE SERIOUS TRAINER

In advanced dog training, and for that matter intermediate training, certain equipment is required to continue your dog's progress. Here are a few items I believe have a place in any serious training program and that are necessary for many training techniques described in this book.

Remote-Controlled Bird Releaser

This handy device can be used in many areas. It is especially helpful in teaching upland skills, because you can release birds at the opportune time while your dog scours the area.

A remote-controlled bird releaser is handy for many tasks.

A bird thrower is especially helpful during multiple-retrieve training.

It's also handy for assisting young dogs to complete blind retrieves over water. Simply place the releaser on the far shoreline and, if your dog struggles, release the bird as a visual cue for your dog to key on.

Remote-Controlled Bird Launcher/Thrower

Along those lines, a remote-controlled bird thrower will help you during multiple-retrieve training, especially if you don't have a helper available. The remote transmitter can control several releasers and toss single, double or triple retrieves — whatever configuration you want. This lets you train your dog to complete advanced marked retrieve patterns, which are discussed in-depth in Chapter 5.

Handheld Dummy Launcher

This tool lets you drill very long marked retrieves without assistance from a helper. It also provides the report of a .22 blank, which will excite your dog just enough to test his steadiness.

Platforms

As with the basic training described in *Tom Dokken's Retriever Training*, the use of platforms is essential to advanced work. We'll use them in variety of drills, from upland work to reinforcing steadiness and hand-signal training.

Knee-High Rubber Boots

Such footwear is essential for teaching your dog to trail a running bird through the uplands. Rubber boots mask your scent, ensuring your dog focuses on trailing bird scent rather than yours.

Standard Training Equipment

Basic, essential equipment includes a 30-foot check cord, heeling stick, remote training collar, 6-foot leash and a fetching stick. Given that you've read the first book, you should already have this gear, which we'll now take to a higher level.

Visual Markers

We'll use two visual aids in this book: white markers/flags that we intend for your dog to see and orange markers that we do not intend for the dog to see. The white markers will help your dog visually catch on to a variety of advanced retrieving drills at a faster pace. Orange markers, on the other hand, are essentially invisible to your dog. They'll help you remember where you planted blind retrieves to more easily direct your dog to them.

You'll also need rubber boots, a check cord, a fetching stick, white markers, orange markers and, of course, a leash.

Other essentials include a blank pistol, heeling stick and remote collar unit (top); a dog blind (below); and a layout blind (Page 15).

Dog Blind and Layout Blind

Given the popularity of field-hunting for waterfowl, we will discuss how to train your dog so he understands his role in actual hunting situations.

Life-Size Goose Dummy

I'm a firm believer that your dog should train with dummies that duplicate the size of the birds you intend for him to retrieve. If you don't practice with a goose-sized dummy, your dog's first goose could prove a real blow to his confidence.

Diving Duck Dummy

This piece of equipment will help you teach your dog to aggressively chase down diving, crippled ducks and stay the course until he makes the retrieve.

Remote Transmitter Shotgun Mount

Another great piece of equipment, especially to reinforce steadiness, is a mount that attaches your remote collar transmitter to the side of your shotgun. Your dog is most likely to become overexcited and break as you stand and shoot. Unfortunately, it can be difficult to correct the dog at that instant because your hands are full. With a transmitter mount, you can quickly administer correction simply by extending your thumb.

Conclusion

It's very important that you have this training equipment before you progress with the advanced training described in this book. In doing so, you'll get the best out of your dog without having to slow down simply because you lack the appropriate gear.

–2–

ADVANCED OBEDIENCE & FORCE FETCH

This chapter reviews and expands upon the training principles described in my first book. Sometimes as trainers, as is also the case with dogs, it's important to take a step back and recall what we've learned. However, the review won't last long. If this is your first stab at dog training, I strongly advise you to read my first book before proceeding.

Obedience Tools

In my training program, there are four training tools that are not optional: the leash, heeling stick, check cord and, probably most important, the e-collar. Their basic use was described in the first book, but they are even more essential now that we'll embark on advanced drills. Precise obedience is absolutely critical to success at this stage in the game.

Throughout the drills described in this chapter, be sure to use these tools to reinforce proper heeling, sitting, staying, coming and other basic commands (your dog should already be very familiar with these concepts). Note that the check cord is used in conjunction with all drills in Chapter 2.

Casting Drills

At this point, your dog is force-fetched, and he has a firm grasp on the place command and other basic obedience requirements. He's ready to learn a skill that will lay much of the foundation for the advanced training to come: casting.

Step 1 is introducing the back cast. We begin here because later we will train the dog to tackle blind retrieves. And in a blind-retrieve scenario, it's always much harder to get the dog to cast back farther away from you than to cast left or right. It's also much easier to call in a dog that's overshot a blind mark than to push him deeper. Therefore the back command is emphasized from the get-go and will be re-emphasized throughout the training process.

Before starting casting drills, be sure your dog is force-fetched and has a firm grasp of other basic obedience requirements.

To teach the back cast, use this simple drill. Position two platforms in front of you about six feet apart. Command "place," and get the dog familiar with the first platform. When that's established, cast right to the other platform, and then cast to the other platform, gradually moving yourself to the back-cast position.

Command "place" while raising your hand over your head, and use the heeling stick to push your dog to the second platform. After the dog is performing this task, you can add in the "back" command.

When your dog is ready, transition to angle-cast drills. Stagger three platforms: one in front, one angled away from you to the right and one away from you to the left, creating a V.

To teach the right- and left-hand back-cast, raise your right hand as you step to the right, and command "back." Let the dog sit on the right-hand platform, and then call him back. Next, repeat the drill to the left platform.

Most dogs can master the right- and left-hand back-cast concept in a day or two.

After your dog has the right- and left-hand back-cast concept down, it's time to move on.

Basic Baseball Diamond

From there, we can move on to the basic baseball diamond, which we'll use to teach the dog the difference between casting right, back and left. The dog is positioned on a platform at the "pitcher's mound," and other platforms are at first, second and third base. Keep the diamond very small. Bases should only be about 10 yards from the pitcher's mound. After all, if the dog can't execute basic casts at close range, how can you ever expect him to handle for you on long retrieves? And you want to be close to the dog in case he gets confused or makes a mistake. It would be counterproductive to spend your morning running 100 yards every two seconds because your dog is struggling. So, let's establish the fundamentals.

Begin by casting the dog back to second base to ensure, first and foremost, that the dog understands the ever-important back cast. Let him sit on second for a moment, and then whistle him back to the pitcher's mound.

The basic baseball diamond drill teaches the dog the difference between casting right, back and left.

The dog is positioned on a platform at the pitcher's mound, and other platforms are at first, second and third base.

This time, let's send him to first base. Take a few steps toward first, cast him toward it with your right hand and give him the place command. Don't be afraid to overemphasize what direction you want the dog to go by continuing to walk toward the platform. Make it easily understood. If you're going to second base, walk toward the pitcher's mound, and push the dog back with the back cast. If the dog makes a mistake, use the check cord to gently stop him and guide him to where you want him to go. It would be foolish to administer corrections to the dog at this stage, because you just gave him three different places to go. Who could expect him to get it perfectly on the first try? Don't put unnecessary pressure on the dog when he's learning something new, but rather make it easy for him to understand and succeed.

Now, you've just given the dog a right-hand cast to first base. Always follow that up by sending him back to second base to keep the back cast fresh. Then you can cast him to third base, back to second, over to first and so on. But always send him to second on every other cast. As an additional reinforcement, I always finish the drill on several back casts in a row to second base. If your dog has problems with three bases, eliminate first or third base, and then add them back in as your dog catches on.

Next, we'll add a small wrinkle. Rather than starting the dog at the pitcher's mound, begin with him at your side a couple of yards in the direction of home plate. Next, command "place" to send him to the pitcher's mound, have him sit on the mound for a couple of seconds, and commence the drill as before.

Each time you send him to a base, call him back to your side and send him to the pitcher's mound. This might seem monotonous (and frankly, the training in future chapters will be more exciting for dog and trainer), but you're preparing the dog for the day when he'll start at your side and be sent on a blind retrieve.

Finish this drill by removing the pitcher's mound platform and running the pattern with the check cord to stop the dog at the pitcher's mound.

Introduction of Dummies

So, the dog will leave your side to go to the pitcher's mound and cast right, left and back. Note that at this point in the curriculum, your dog must be force-fetched to proceed. He has to know that when you tell him to fetch a dummy, it's a demand, not a request. If his force-fetch training has slipped in the least, have him do a few stacks of dummies as described in the force-fetch section of book No. 1.

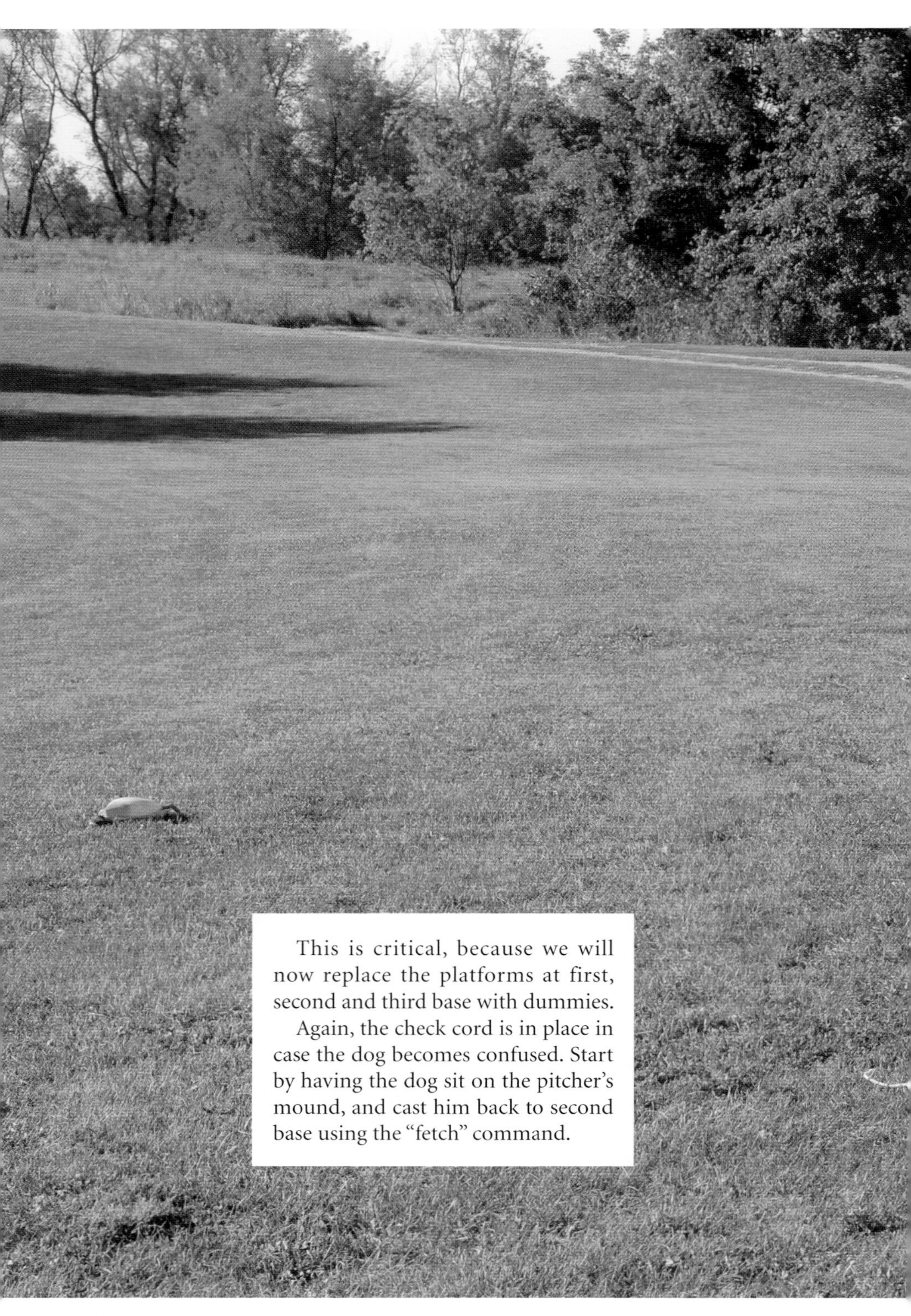

This is critical, because we will now replace the platforms at first, second and third base with dummies.

Again, the check cord is in place in case the dog becomes confused. Start by having the dog sit on the pitcher's mound, and cast him back to second base using the "fetch" command.

If he delivers the dummy to hand, you can send him to first or third, but always remember to send him back to second after every left or right cast.

If he executes the drill with ease right away, great. However, some dogs might struggle a bit. If that's the case, start with dummies exclusively on second base, and just drill the back cast. Then you can add dummies to first base and ultimately third. Don't worry if the dog is confused — it just means you need to take a step back and simplify. He'll get it. If your dog has problems, go back to using your check cord to help the dog out.

SITTING TO A WHISTLE BLAST

As part of the next step, you'll be using a whistle blast to command your dog to sit. Don't overthink this step. He already knows sit and place, right? So just begin incorporating the whistle blast into all of the drills described in this chapter. For example, whenever your dog reaches a platform, give him the verbal "sit" command, give one whistle blast and follow it up with another verbal "sit" command. Gradually, you can go to one verbal command with a whistle blast, and before long, your dog will sit right down after one quick whistle blast. It's an easy adjustment that most dogs will quickly pick up on.

When you're confident the dog thoroughly understands baseball casts with dummies and he's making few mistakes, return to having the dog start at your side. Send him to the pitcher's mound, have him sit and start your casting sequence. If necessary, you can go back to having him start on the mound, but with consistent repetition and check cord assistance, he should be a regular Mickey Mantle in no time.

The Wagon Wheel

OK, time to move on and start a drill called the wagon wheel. Because we're teaching the dog something new, we'll go back to using platforms instead of dummies. Position them just three or four yards away from you and the dog at 12 o'clock, 3 o'clock, 6 o'clock and 9 o'clock. (Can you see how this drill got its name?)

With the dog sitting at your side, put your hand in front his nose toward the platform of your choice and command "place." Help guide the dog using the check cord if necessary, but insist he goes where you say. In this drill, you are directing the dog from your side, not casting him right or left. That's a critical difference between the wagon wheel and the baseball drill.

Let the dog sit on the platform for a few seconds, and then call him back to your side, turn and send him to a new platform. At first, it might be easiest and least confusing for the dog if you send him in the opposite direction from which he was just sent. That way, he won't be tempted to go back to the preceding platform. Most dogs should accomplish this drill rather easily because the platforms are so close.

When completed, all we're going to do is replace each platform with a dummy. Use the fetch command to send the dog for the dummy of your choice. When he delivers it, toss the dummy back to the same spot. Then, tell your dog "no," turn 180 degrees and have

him fetch the dummy on the other side. By turning away from the dummy you just tossed, which the dog no doubt would love to retrieve, you're helping him to understand it's not the one you want. He's likely to slightly refuse to move from the dummy you just tossed — and that's OK — but you need to stay on your toes and anticipate those mistakes. If he refuses to turn or attempts to fetch the wrong dummy, stop him abruptly with the check cord, move him to heel and have him fetch the correct dummy. If the dog struggles, just move a step closer to the dummy you want, or remove the dummies at the 3 and 9 o'clock positions so only two dummies are in the picture. It never hurts to simplify the drill to help the dog succeed. A major mistake many people make is believing that their dogs are stubborn or trying to test them, when 99 percent of the time, the poor dogs are just confused or were rushed into an overly difficult drill. Unfortunately, when people think their dogs are being stubborn, their instinct is to discipline the dog, and inevitably the dog decides it hates training. So simplify, and don't put pressure on the dog. We teach first and then reinforce.

When your dog successfully fetches the second dummy, again toss it back, tell him "no," and turn 180 degrees. It's very important that when you turn, the dog moves with you obediently at heel. Make sure it's clear that you determine which direction to turn and which dummy to fetch, not the dog. He's already been taught obedience at heel (or should have been), so just reinforce it with the check cord or heeling stick. To keep his heel work sharp, make sure you don't pivot around in the same direction every time. Pivot right, and other times pivot left, so the dog gets used to readjusting himself both ways as you turn.

Eight-Dummy Wagon Wheel

You'll know your dog has really caught on to the wagon wheel when you can toss a dummy, say "no," and he's already begun to turn and look for another to fetch. At that point, you can expand on the drill with an outer wheel of dummies that's two or three yards beyond the inner wheel. Place four dummies in the outer wheel: one in the gap between 3 and 6 o'clock, one between 6 and 9 o'clock and so on. A total of eight dummies are used.

To accomplish this exercise, the dog must run through a gap between two dummies, ignore his instinct to pick one of them up, and continue on to the outer circle to pick up the dummy you want. For the first few retrieves, actually stand in the gap between the two dummies in the inner wheel, which helps make it extra clear to the dog that you want him to fetch a dummy in the outer wheel. Guide him with the check cord if necessary. When he brings the dummy back to you, toss it back to its position, turn 180 degrees, move to the opposite gap, and have him fetch that dummy. At this stage, don't have your dog fetch any inner-wheel dummies. As his understanding of the drill improves, you can begin inching

farther away from the gap until ultimately you're standing in the center of the wheel, sending the dog for a retrieve through the inner gap.

As with the other foundational drills in Chapter 2, the eight-dummy wagon wheel prepares the dog for blind-retrieve training. Later, when you line him up for a blind, you want him paying attention to where your hand is at, not looking out into the field or becoming otherwise distracted. It's important to teach the dog to take a direct line from your hand. He shouldn't care what lies to the left or right of that path.

Soon, the dog will reliably run through gaps in the inner wheel to retrieve dummies in the outer wheel. At this point, he's ready to begin fetching inner-wheel dummies as well. So

mix it up. Send him to outer dummies, inner dummies or whatever combination you like. The dog will learn to focus closely on your hand to differentiate which dummy you want, and this concentration and teamwork will pay dividends down the road. Be ready for any confusion so you can help the dog through it. When you start adding inner dummies, your dog will be even more tempted to stop for one en route to an outer dummy.

As the dog learns to perform the drill with ease at close proximity, you can begin extending it to increase the challenge. Creep it out slowly, just a few yards at a time. If the dog continues to progress, you can eventually extend the inner wheel to 10 yards and the outer wheel to 20.

Long Baseball Diamond

After your dog has mastered the basic baseball pattern and wagon-wheel drill, he is ready for the next stage in training: a larger, more advanced baseball drill. You need a short-grass field of fairly large acreage to accomplish this, and ideally it will be the same field you used for the basic baseball diamond. The canine memory is very location-based. It's easier for dogs to learn and remember training that took place in the same spot. Your dog is like a child who can do algebra in the classroom he was taught but not in the room next door.

So, let's get into some more advanced work, which means going back to the use of platforms rather than dummies. Extend the baseball field by moving each base/platform five to 10 yards farther away from the pitcher's mound, and backing up five to 10 yards to increase the distance the dog must travel from your side to the mound. Gradually increase these distances in 10-yard increments during a two- to three-

week period until the distance from the mound to your side and from the mound to the bases is 70 to 80 yards. White markers will make this drill go faster. It's OK to take longer than two to three weeks or to take a step back if the dog struggles, but that's a loose timeline based on my experience with many retrievers.

When the dog is leaving your side, running 80 yards just to reach the pitcher's mound, and running another 80 yards to reach a base, you're

ready to swap out the platforms for dummies. Have him retrieve them just as before, but make sure he does so with obedience and consistency. This drill is hugely important, and it's one you should constantly go back and review throughout the dog's life to keep his hand signals sharp. The ability to take a hand signal during hunting or field trial conditions has nothing to do with the dog's ability. It's all about repetition and practice with a dedicated trainer.

Double T

The next step is just a matter of adding a few new positions to the baseball diamond where we can send the dog to fine-tune his casting abilities. Because we've further complicated the drill, we return temporarily to platforms. All we're going to do is add a first base, third base and pitcher's mound inside our larger, normal baseball pattern. This allows us to use various combinations of hand signals.

However, first you need to show the dog the new positions, so walk him over to the new inner first and third bases, and command place before you begin. That's usually all he'll need to recognize them. After that, take your position in the drill, and send the dog to the first pitcher's mound. Cast him to a base, let him sit a couple of seconds and call him in. Initially, you will have platforms at both pitchers mounds, so the dog will always want to stop at the first platform, and you'll have to push him back if you want him to go to the second one. However, when the dog shows competency with the drill, we will remove the platforms from the pitchers' mounds. At this point, you can use a whistle blast to stop the dog at the first mound or allow him to run freely through the center until your whistle blast stops him at the second mound. It's an added layer of obedience and control. The dog no longer runs to a platform, he runs until you tell him to stop.

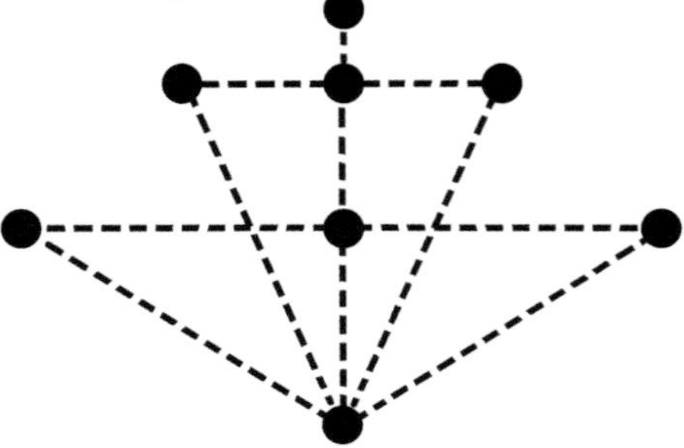

Above is an overhead view of the Double T drill pattern.

As a final step, replace all base platforms with retrieving dummies, and run the drill accordingly.

Congratulations. Your dog has already achieved a level of training that many retrievers never reach. But don't pat yourself on the back for too long. We'll revisit these drills throughout the rest of your dog's long and fruitful hunting career, but we're about to get really advanced. Your dog is up for it — are you?

Water Baseball

For our next drill, we're basically going to set up a water version of the baseball drill (pictured starting on Page 86). The ideal pond is about 30 yards across and fairly square in shape. Position first, second and third bases along the shoreline. This version of the drill is more difficult than on land, so put white markers at each base to help your dog understand. Additionally, be sure to show the dog where each base is simply by walking him around the perimeter of the pond.

Start the drill by giving the dog a "back" toward second base. Because he's already run white markers over water, he should have no trouble completing the retrieve.

For the next retrieve, it's critical that you've kept up with your obedience training. Again, direct the dog toward second base, but stop him with a whistle blast when he's halfway there, and cast him left or right to pick up a dummy at first or third. There's no pitcher's mound with T-markers, so this is how you'll cast the dog left or right. Just as with the original baseball drill, remember to send the dog to second base on every other retrieve to reinforce going back and to instill confidence.

The final step in this drill is to remove the white markers, and run it as prescribed.

—3—

LINING DRILLS & ADVANCED BACK COMMAND

Every drill we cover in this book teaches the dog an important lesson, but of equal importance, you're also establishing trust with the dog. If you're consistent with his training, it furthers the bond you share. Your dog will see you as a trustworthy and fair leader, and you'll be rewarded with his loyalty, affection and desire to please.

At no time is this truer than when we get into lining drills. In this chapter, we will teach the dog that every time we sit him down at our side, put our hand in front of his nose and give him a line, he can be 100 percent sure there's a bird or dummy out there for him. In time, he'll be just as confident it's there as if he'd seen it fall — because he trusts you — and he'll know that by following your guidance, he'll be rewarded with a dummy or bird. A dog that comes to this revelation will easily transition to taking a nice, long line through land or water en route to a blind retrieve.

White Marker Lining Drills

As in casting drills, lining drills begin with a white marker. The marker can be anything from a white bucket, a white flag or a windsock on a pole. It just needs to be white and stick up a few feet off the ground to ensure it's nice and visible for the dog. Position your white marker in a big, open field — athletic fields are perfect. Keep in mind you will eventually need at least 250 yards of space as the drill progresses.

Before we begin, it's important to note that we're about to teach your dog to take a long line to a fall, but many amateur trainers at this stage are still primarily just tossing dummies for their dogs to fetch. And a dummy can only be tossed about 30 yards or so. That's a problem, because if all the dog ever does is fetch 30-yard dummies, he starts to assume that every bird or dummy has fallen about 30 yards away. Then one day while pheasant hunting, you lightly hit a rooster that coasts down 80 yards away. Guess what: The dog might have seen it fall, but he's likely to stop and start hunting after 30 to 40 yards. It's not his fault. That distance has been drilled into him.

But we're going to teach your dog the right way. We want him always thinking "long." We will convince him that the bird is always a little farther away than it appears. As we touched on the previous chapter, it's very easy to call a dog back in and direct him to the bird with hand signals. It's not easy to get a reluctant dog to cast farther from us.

So, let's introduce the white marker. Walk the dog out with you into the field, position the white marker, and have the dog sit and stay 15 yards from it. Then, allowing the dog to see you, put a half-dozen dummies by the marker. The marker will serve as a point of reference for the dog, helping him find the dummies as we gradually increase the distance he must travel to find them.

When the dummies are in position, walk your dog at heel 15 yards away from them. Put your hand in front of his nose toward the marker/dummies, and command "back." You can use the fetch command if he's confused, but you should definitely begin transitioning to back at this stage. As the dog is about to pick up a dummy, begin walking backward. For the second retrieve, you want to be an additional 15 yards from the marker. Then repeat the process: Give him a back, and walk backward another 15 yards. Each time the dog completes a retrieve without issue, increase the distance. Your goal on the first day is to send the dog for the sixth retrieve from a distance of about 50 yards.

The next day, position your white marker in the exact spot as on Day 1 to be consistent and avoid confusion. Sit the dog down 25 yards from the marker, and let him see you drop half a dozen dummies by it. Give him a back, and increase the distance by 15 to 20 yards for the second retrieve. Continue to increase the distance for each retrieve in 15- to 20-yard increments. Provided that Day 1 was a success, your goal for the sixth and final retrieve of Day 2 is 100 yards. However, if the dog struggles, there's no need to rush him. Just move back up, and repeat the drill. Ensure you finish your day on a successful note. Doing so will keep your dog's confidence in you and himself high.

On Day 3, you'll again position the marker in the same spot and drop the dummies by it as your dog observes, this time from 75 yards away. Then run the drill as prescribed. Your goal for Day 3 is to finish 150 yards away.

Always begin this drill about 25 yards closer to the marker than you finished the previous day, and work your way back out. Your goal for Day 4 is to finish 200 yards out, and your goal for Day 5 is 225 yards. Ultimately, on Day 6, the goal is a 250-yard retrieve.

However, when you're out to 200 yards and beyond, there's no sense in having the dog complete six retrieves. Even for a fit retriever, that's a lot of running. Just have your dog complete a couple of retrieves at that distance.

When the dog is running this drill at 250 yards, you should also no longer have to let him see you put the dummies out. He's smart enough to recognize that where there's a white marker, there's a dummy — especially if, as advised, you put the marker in the same spot every time.

The next step is simply to remove the marker, position the dummies in the same spot and start the process again. Start at 50 yards, give the dog a line, and every time he successfully completes a retrieve without struggling, you can move back another 50 yards. All you're doing is relying on the dog's memory rather than the marker's visual cue. Take your time, and train this step during the course of a few days, if necessary, until the dog has no trouble completing it at 250 yards.

When he'll do so flawlessly, you're ready to set up the drill in another training area. As we're in a new location, your dog won't know where the pile of dummies is, so we start again from scratch. Sit the dog down 15 yards away, position the white marker, let him see you add the dummies and run the drill. When he'll take a 250-yard line to the pile of dummies with no marker, it's time to establish another new training location. Your goal is to run this drill in several new locations one at a time until you have a half-dozen areas for your dog to run lines. Each time you add a new area, go back and review the others to keep them fresh in your dog's mind. And remember, always use the white marker to keep the dog's confidence sky high when you start off in a new, unfamiliar location.

Why teach the dog to run the same drill in a variety of fields? You want the dog to start to grasp that a command means the same thing regardless of where he's at. If you only train in one location, one day you'll give your dog a line somewhere new, and he'll say to himself, "I don't know what to do. This isn't my spot. It doesn't even look like anything I've seen before." That's the canine mentality, so a location change can be confusing. Therefore, when you select training areas to run lines, it's also important to select places with different terrain features and other physical aspects. Perhaps one has small hills, another has a pond off to the side or some other little nuance. The more variety, the better. That way, ultimately, when your dog gets to his first blind, he'll think, "Well, I haven't been here before, but it looks a little like spot No. 3. Let's do this!" He'll be confident in what you've taught him and ready to roll.

Water Lines with White Markers

The next step in the white-marker curriculum is introducing the dog to lining drills over water. A critical difference is that unless you can walk on water, you won't be able to start near the marker and gradually work away from it. Instead, start with a small pond that's perhaps 25 to 30 yards across — nothing too challenging at this point. Put your marker on the opposite shoreline, and show the dog that you're adding a pile of dummies next to it. Then give the dog a line, and send him across the pond to the marker. Remember, keep it simple. We want this to be an easy swim. The ideal pond is oval-shaped or rectangular, so you can stand near the middle and the dog isn't tempted to run around the edge rather than swim.

When the dog is ready to be further challenged, find a larger pond in the 50- to 75-yard range. On land, it's easy to help a confused dog reach the marker, but in a pond, even Michael Phelps would have difficulty lending the dog any assistance. So enlist a training partner who'll help you encourage the dog across. For the first few retrieves, have the helper stand next to the marker and wave a dummy. When he has the pup's attention, send your dog. As long as your buddy continues waving the dummy, the dog should happily continue across the pond. However, if the dog needs further enticement, have your buddy toss a dummy onto the pile, and call to the dog — whatever it takes to get him across the pond and to the dummies. As the dog begins to grasp what's expected of him, you can have your helper sit down or hide in the brush. If the dog continues to succeed, the helper stays hidden. If not, the helper can step back out and resume assisting the dog.

The rest of the exercise mirrors the land-lines drill. Remove the markers, and have the dog run lines across the pond using his memory. If he struggles, go back to running the drill with your marker. Otherwise, find a new pond to run lines, initially with the marker and then without. As with land lines, you want a good half-dozen ponds where you can run lines, and you should always go back and revisit your other lines after establishing a new one to keep the dog's confidence up. The more ponds you have to run lines, the better, because that helps assure the dog that every time you give him a line, a reward awaits his swim.

HOW TO HELP A STRUGGLING DOG

As long as you don't rush them, most dogs will start to grasp the white-marker concept within the first couple of days. However, some won't, and this is no big deal as long as you handle it appropriately. You need to keep the young dog's confidence high (a natural lack of confidence could be what's affecting the dog's ability to learn in the first place), which we'll accomplish by further simplifying the drill for the dog.

Begin by setting up your white marker and dummy pile as you would normally, but in this modified version of the drill, you'll have a helper stand near the dummy pile waving a dummy in his hand. When the helper has your dog's attention, send the dog to the marker. If the dog requires further encouragement, the helper can even toss a dummy next to the marker or yell, "Hey, hey, hey!" to keep the dog on course. After a few successful retrieves, try the drill without the helper. It's that simple.

Land-Water-Land Transition

However, you can't just place all of your dog's water lines at the edge of the opposing shoreline, or one day you'll drop a duck well onto land, and your dog will insist on hunting the shoreline. Even if you try to push him back with hand signals, he'll continue cruising the bank. And why shouldn't he? That's where all of his birds have ever been. He's accustomed to finding them there and supremely confident he can do so again if he just keeps trying.

So let's teach the dog that sometimes when we give him a line, he'll need to drive through the water and continue his surge onto land. You can use a white marker and possibly a helper to assist your dog in continuing on to the dummy, but it is essential that you include this type of retrieve in your training regimen.

Multiple Line Markers

To clue the dog into what's expected of him in our next drill, it should be set up in a field where you've run lines before. To help visualize the setup for multiple line markers, imagine you're standing on a pitcher's mound looking into the outfield. We will position white markers and dummies at left, right and center field, about 150 to 200 yards away. Show the dog where the markers are, return to the pitcher's mound and have the dog sit. Give him a line, taking the time to make absolutely certain he's looking at the same marker you are, and send him for the retrieve. When he's doing well, you guessed it, remove the markers, and repeat the drill, forcing the dog to use his memory and the direction of his cast to be successful.

Just like that, the dog has connected the dots between the lining/white-marker drills and drills such as the wagon wheel from Chapter 1. He's one step closer to attempting his first blind retrieve.

Inline Mark and Line Combination

The ball of mallards swings wide of the decoys and then hooks back into the wind for a final approach to your spread. Your young black Lab is rock solid on his platform as you ease the 12-gauge to your shoulder. Your first shot drops a duck cleanly right over the decoys; your second clips a drake through the primaries, and it manages to fly 150 yards before splashing into the lake. The first duck is an easy retrieve, but your inexperienced dog never saw the second. Can you handle him to it?

This is a frequent hunting scenario, but it can also be very challenging for your dog, unless you've gone through the training to help him overcome it. He should have little trouble fetching the first duck, but he's likely to have a hard time accepting your handling to reach the distant second bird. Why? At this stage in your dog's training, 99 percent of the time, he'll go right back to the location of the initial fall (the one he saw) and start hunting, even if he's already brought the first duck back to you. Retrievers instinctively just can't leave the spot alone where they know they saw a duck drop. Your goal is to teach him to forget about the marked fall or other distraction and choose instead to pay attention to your handling. In turn, he'll be rewarded. Note how the wagon wheel introduced him to this concept. We will now build upon it.

As nearly always when teaching something new and somewhat complex, we begin in the yard. Start with a stack of dummies about 25 yards away. Make sure the dog can see them, so he'll readily fetch one with every back. After a few retrieves, toss a dummy five or six yards in front of you, and say the dog's name to send him for it. After its delivery, give the dog a back toward the stack of dummies. He'll have to run right through the location of the thrown fall, and he will say to himself, "OK, I just got a short retrieve. Now I have to run all the way past where it fell for another dummy."

You just taught your dog the basics of the drill. Next we'll extend it at one of our long-lines locations. But first, be honest with yourself: As your dog progressed throughout this chapter, did you take the time to revisit his lining drills, or did you get lazy? If the former is true, great, he's ready to tackle the next phase. If not, go back and review. That skill set needs to be fresh in his mind, because he'll use the lining drill and build upon it during this next phase.

Begin in a field where the dog has run long lines dozens of times and is confident in himself. Set up your pile of dummies, say "dead bird" (a command I like to introduce at this stage) and give the dog a line. At this point, as far as the dog is concerned, he's just running lines. When he returns with a dummy, however, things change.

Next, we'll advance the exercise with the help of a friend. Have your helper stand 40 yards off to the side (right or left, it doesn't matter) of the imaginary line leading from you and your dog to the pile of bumpers. In this scenario, your helper tosses a dummy or bird such as a pigeon for the dog to retrieve after each successfully completed long line. You need to use birds for your long lines, too, so that the reward for both retrieves is equal. It's much more exciting for the dog to retrieve a nice, feathered bird than a plain old hunk of plastic.

The introduction of the helper further distracts the dog from the long line, thereby increasing the demand on his concentration and focus. Again, we're teaching the dog that when you give him a line, he has to block everything else from his mind and focus on your hand. A final distraction you can add to this drill is having your helper fire a blank gun or a shotgun as he tosses a bird or dummy. The sound will further tempt your dog to stop and hunt the location of the marked fall when it's time for him to run the long line. Some dogs will even start to run toward the location where they heard the shot echo, perhaps in a clump of trees nearby. Be prepared for these mistakes so you can quickly and calmly help your dog through it. If the dog has trouble at any stage in this drill, even before the introduction of your helper, don't be afraid to use hand signals to help him and reinforce where you want him to go.

Finally, a point of clarification: Don't confuse a blind retrieve with the long lines your dog is running in this drill. We haven't yet introduced the blind retrieve, although we are preparing the dog for that eventuality. These long lines rely upon the dog's memory to help guide him to the stack of dummies. As we continue to advance your dog's skills (and those of his trainer), it's important that you can make this distinction. Otherwise, my system might confuse you. And if you're confused, guess what that spells for your pup.

If your dog skillfully executes the inline mark/line combo drill, that's a really good sign, because to do so demonstrates a mastery of nearly everything we've trained for to this point. He's ready to move on to his first blind retrieve.

Pick up the dummy your helper has thrown first.

Then send your dog using the "back" command to the memory line.

–4–

FIRST BLIND RETRIEVE

The bluebills rocket into your decoys the way only speedy little divers can, and the possibility of finishing off your limit flashes through your mind as you rise to shoot. Your first shot is true, so you swing through a second drake, intent on doubling. You hit the duck but not well, and it continues for 200 yards before petering out. Your yellow Lab never saw it drop. You'll have to hope his training to that point has been enough to help him reach the fleeing bird. Can he complete his first blind retrieve during an actual hunt?

With eager anticipation, you give him a "back," and he leaps from the blind, creating a substantial wake with his charging entry. After 100 yards, he's breaking a thin layer of ice with every stroke. You blow your whistle, and he turns and looks for directions. You direct him to the bird.

"Come on, come on," you quietly cheer him on from the blind.

As he nears the duck, it flaps a wing in an effort to escape — he sees it! — and your Lab's in hot pursuit. The bluebill dives. Your dog circles. And after the duck's fourth dive, he grabs it. You lay on the praise as he reaches the blind, content that your training efforts have all been worth it thanks to the memory you'll now cherish.

My friends, that kind of effort and skill is what separates a duck dog from a mere pet. The ability to make a blind retrieve is the hallmark of a well-trained, talented retriever. If your dog can execute one, he'll be a better conservation tool, and you'll be party to one of the most exciting experiences a dog guy can have.

But it doesn't just happen on its own. Retrievers can be pretty darn good hunting dogs based on their inherent instincts alone, but they must be taught to take blinds. Here's how to do that.

It is mandatory before proceeding that your dog has done all of his white-marker lines, memory lines and hand-signal drills on land and water. Those training scenarios were almost as much about building the dog's confidence going into blinds as they were about teaching obedience. After all, as long as you took your time, the dog knew where the dummies were. However, that's about to change, so it's good to enter this new phase with the dog's confidence riding high.

Begin by finding a grass field that's no longer than 6 inches high — nothing too thick and challenging, just enough to hide a bird — because we want to set the dog up for success on his first blind re-

trieve. That's really important, because if the dog doesn't complete it, he's going to say to himself, "Well, this is just too tough. I can't do it." That's a major setback.

Along that line, it's also crucial to determine the wind direction. Many people think it's best to set up the dog's first blind retrieve into the wind, figuring the wind will help carry the bird's scent to the dog. However, when the wind is in your dog's face, he actually has a natural tendency to stop short of the retrieve and start quartering against the wind. Most young dogs will therefore

refuse to run deep enough with the wind in their faces.

I've found that the best way to set up for a blind-retrieve introduction is with a crosswind blowing right to left or left to right. That makes it far easier for your dog to find one of the birds in the scenario we're about to diagram.

Yes, "birds," not just "bird." Scatter several of them across the field, because above all else, your dog must succeed. He must return to your side, head held high, proudly carrying a bird. So boost the odds by arranging a line of birds about 75 yards away from

where you'll send the dog. Every 20 yards along the line, place a bird. Basically, we want to guarantee that your dog finds one. This is called salting the area with birds. Think about it: If you have four or five birds in a line across the field, you've got about 100 yards covered. Given the crosswind, all your dog has to do is run through the line of birds, and he'll find one. It's by far best to use frozen pigeons or ducks rather than dummies, because their stronger scent further ensures your dog's success. It's important to use orange flags to mark the ends of your line of birds.

OK, it's go time. Line up your dog, and command, "Dead bird, back!" He'll take off, but he really isn't sure where he's going. Fortunately, all you have to do is get him to run through that 100-yard window where he'll smell a bird and pick it up.

Even though you've set your dog up to succeed, it will likely prove necessary for you to stop him and give him hand signals a few times. Keep in mind that this drill is foreign to him, so his hand signals won't be as sharp and crisp as normal. That's OK, they don't have to be at this point. This initial blind doesn't need to be a thing of beauty. Your goal is simply to hack the dog downwind of a bird.

Similarly, you also might not — in fact, you probably won't — get as good an initial back cast from the dog as you'd like. In that event, just slowly walk forward behind the dog as he goes to help push him toward your line of pigeons.

Find New Fields

It's important to run blinds in a variety of fields, because if your dog grows accustomed to a field and can rely on his memory, he isn't truly running blind retrieves. So find new, unfamiliar locations.

And keep in mind that if you give your dog a “back” in the opposite direction at a field you’ve been using, this can count as a new area, because the dog won’t know where the bird is at.

Water Blinds

As with land blinds, we don't expect your dog to make a 200-yard water blind on his first try. Instead you want to start with a small pond that's 40 to 50 yards across. Again, the wind is everything, so ensure your dog has a crosswind to work with.

After you determine a spot from which to send your dog, salt the opposite bank with pigeons or ducks, spaced out just as we did on land. Ideally, you should have a helper on the opposite shore who can call to your dog and encourage him across the pond in case he struggles. If all else fails, your helper can even toss a bird and allow the dog to see the splash — whatever it takes to ensure the dog completes a retrieve, even if it doesn't work out according to the script. An alternative to using a helper, if your pond is shallow

enough for wading, is walking out behind the dog and pushing him along as we did on land.

OK, you're all set. Give the dog a line, and command back to send him across the pond. If he stops or wavers off course, have your helper step in and help. Fortunately, at this point, based on your dog's level of training, he'll likely have enough confidence to swim your small pond to find one of the birds.

Advanced Blinds

When a retriever is running blinds, a lot of trainers think the dog has graduated from running long lines, and they quit doing them. This is a huge mistake. No matter how many blinds you run, it's long lines that keep your dog's hand signals and other handling sharp.

So continue running long lines as your blinds training progresses. Speaking of which, how's your pup doing? Is he charging away from you with increasing confidence toward the salted area? Good, then it's time to reduce the number of birds by one half. If he's still succeeding after a couple of days, remove half of those.

The next step is a big one: It's time to completely remove your dog's safety net and move on to single-bird blinds. Place a bird in a downwind field (wind at your back), and put a subtle orange marker next to it for your reference. You do not want the dog to notice the marker. Otherwise, a smart retriever will start to key on it, and then you're just running the white-marker drill again.

We set up a crosswind scenario earlier so all the dog had to do was run through our salted line of birds to smell one. However, with just one bird in the field, it's all the more important to keep the dog on course, and a downwind tends to be the easiest to accomplish that task. As we noted, the dog doesn't really want to run into the wind, so he's likely to curve or drift off line and start quartering. If you stop the dog and try to send him back into the wind, he might even show some refusal to take your hand signal. At best, he'll just go a few yards and start hunting again. On the other hand, a crosswind starts out OK, but your dog might drift off course with the wind. At that point you need to stop the dog and cast him back toward the bird — and therefore into the wind — which results in the same aforementioned frustrations. So, we start with the wind at our backs to best ensure the dog takes your cast and stays on line.

Start with retrieves in the 50- to 75-yard range on land and 40- to 50-yard range on water. Help the dog as necessary using the same strategies as when the areas were salted: Use a helper over water, walk toward the bird on land and use hand signals. As your dog's confidence grows, so too will yours, and you can begin to slowly extend the blinds by 20 to 30 yards until your dog will eagerly fetch them out to 250 yards. Just don't rush him or allow him to fail. It's amazing how fast a dog's confidence can sink until pretty soon he starts stopping right in the middle of the retrieve. He just shuts down because he fears failure. That won't happen to your dog, though, because you've just learned how to set him up for success. Your dog won't know how to fail a retrieve or give up on a blind, because he's never going to experience it.

–5–

ADVANCED MARKED RETRIEVES, HONORING & OTHER WATERFOWL SKILLS

After spending the previous day scouting, you and three buddies are hunkered along a hedgerow that you've determined to be the perfect spot to pass-shoot Canada geese. Right on cue, the birds crest the horizon en route from grains fields back to water. They're high, with a blustery wind at their backs, but you're willing to shoot if they pass directly overhead, exposing their breasts for a clean kill.

You pick one out, swing your barrel beyond its outstretched black head and touch the trigger. The goose crumples. The other geese gain speed but err greatly by continuing down the line of hunters. Your buddy on the end shoots a goose through the primaries, and, aided by its momentum and the wind, the goose sails a great distance before finally striking the earth.

Fortunately, your dog saw the goose fall, but this is a challenging retrieve — will he make a hero out of himself?

You might think we're taking a step backward with this chapter on marked falls, given that your dog has already completed a blind retrieve. However, when we get into advanced marked retrieves — the really long ones — we are presenting the dog with an equal challenge. It's easy to spot a retriever that hasn't gone through such lessons. He'll stop short of a long retrieve, convinced there's no way it could've gone any farther, or he'll take his eye off the bird before it drops, because he's convinced it's gotten away. So, let's nip that in the bud before it starts. Here's how to teach your dog that no bird is too far for him.

We begin by extending our single retrieves with the help of a thrower. Set up the drill in a large field, which doesn't need to have more than mowed grass for cover. Start with just a basic 50-yard retrieve. Your thrower's job is to get the dog's attention, by calling, "Hey, hey, hey" or firing a blank pistol as he tosses a dummy. The dummy should be thrown off to the thrower's side, angled away from you, and land

about 20 to 30 yards from the thrower. Send the dog with his name. The retrieve is relatively short, and the cover isn't high, so the dog should fetch the dummy with little difficulty. We aren't working on having the dog run out and start hunting at this stage. You just want a nice, wide-open space where he can quickly fetch thrown dummies.

This drill should go relatively fast, because the dog's already run these distances in earlier lining drills. Therefore, we continue on Day 2 by starting the first retrieve with our thrower 100 yards away. The last retrieve should be at 175.

On Day 3, the dog will probably have a strong grasp of this drill, so you can start at 150 yards and work all the way back to 250.

Don't force your dog into this timeline, however. Most will complete the drill in three days, but don't worry if it takes him an extra few days to accomplish it. Just en-

sure that your dog can make a 250-yard marked retrieve before moving on.

After that's established, you should duplicate the drill in multiple fields with your thrower, just like we did with lining drills and for similar reasons. Your goal is for these new fields to expose the dog to a variety of terrain features and changes.

Then it's simply time to repeat the drill over water. By the time your dog has achieved long marked retrieves on land, it's common that he'll see the thrower across the water, recognize what's expected of him and be willing to complete long water retrieves, as well. Your setup and goals are very similar to land drills, except you cannot extend the drill by simply backing away from the thrower (unless you can walk on water).

You need ponds of various sizes, but fortunately at this point, you should have already found them, given that you've completed lining drills over water. Begin this drill at a pond that's 50 to 60 yards in diameter and, during the course of a few days to a week, graduate to larger ponds until your dog can complete a 250-yarder over water.

Another important consideration is making sure your thrower isn't always throwing the dummies directly onto the shoreline. Have him throw various setups, especially away from the water, so the dog has to run out onto land a ways. Otherwise, your dog will be prone to always hunting the shoreline for his retrieves, despite the fact the duck might have fallen many yards beyond the shore.

Honoring

Many, if not most, people who own retrievers have a hunting partner who also has a dog. Why then do so many people consider honoring to be a nice polishment but not something every dog should be taught? That attitude can present a big problem in a duck hunting situation. I've seen it many times. Often, one owner has a nice, steady retriever that's willing to sit and wait to

be sent, but his friend's dog is not likewise well trained. Most unfortunately, the well-trained dog ends up with the short end of the stick, because as soon as a bird hits the water, guess which dog gets to it first? The unsteady dog breaks, makes the retrieve and the steady dog gets no reward for his good behavior. The dog begins to wonder if it will ever get a chance to retrieve, and eventually, he'll just think, "The heck with it" and start breaking. Therefore, while honoring is typically categorized as an advanced skill, I believe every dog should be taught to do it.

To teach your dog to sit and honor another dog's retrieve, he first must be absolutely rock steady on his own. So go back to the platform drills that we used in my first book. Position the dog on the platform, throw a dummy, and reinforce with an e-collar that he mustn't move until he hears his name. He's elevated, so he should already understand very well what's expected of him.

To teach honoring, you simply add a second platform to the equation with another dog, preferably the buddy's dog that'll accompany you this fall. The platforms should be no more than 10 feet apart. Assuming neither dog has been taught to honor, both should be on leads and wearing remote collars.

Have each dog honor the other dog for several retrieves. Then switch roles, and make the other dog honor for several retrieves.

The next step is to alternate retrieves, no longer using the leash but instead using the remote collar to enforce steadiness.

Next, you or a helper tosses a dummy out in front of the dogs. Both must sit and wait, which you can reinforce with the lead. One handler (you or your buddy) sends Dog A for the retrieve by saying the dog's name, while Dog B honors. It's very important at this stage that the honoring dog is shown it must sit and stay. It's already steady but will likely be tempted to compete with the other dog for the dummy. That's why we have the leash and remote collar on, because many dogs will immediately try to break when they're introduced to this drill. The leash is the ultimate control. If the dog breaks, promptly tug the leash, correct the dog with the collar, and get the dog back in place by commanding him to heel and sit.

Repeat this drill several times, letting Dog A make at least a half-dozen retrieves while you work with Dog B on patiently sitting and watching. The honoring dog will begin to understand that just because a retrieve is thrown doesn't mean he'll be sent for it. After a few repetitions, he should settle down and quit pulling on the leash as Dog A retrieves. Remember, at this point Dog B is working on honoring, not retrieving. He must overcome his jealousy of the other dog getting the retrieve and learn to wait patiently.

Start with hand-thrown dummies. As your weekly sessions progress, you can further tempt the honoring dog by throwing birds with a blank gun, and ultimately a shotgun can be fired with each

retrieve. When you add the gun, you can expect the dogs to try to break again, so be prepared to make corrections.

As your dog shows signs that he understands it's his job to sit and wait, you can take his leash off and rely strictly on the remote collar to reinforce his honor. This is also the point in the lesson when the shoe goes on the other foot: We'll now ask Dog A to honor. Start with him on a lead with the remote collar, and progress through the drill as prescribed.

It's going to take several sessions for these dogs to understand that they must honor while the other dog makes the retrieve. However, we can encourage this learning process. It's important that you end these sessions, including the first one, by rewarding

the honoring dog with a retrieve. By doing so, you teach the dog it has to stay and honor, but also that it'll get a chance to retrieve. Otherwise, even if your dog has strong desire to please, honoring will cause him to wonder what's in it for him. He needs to know a reward awaits his good behavior. Finish this drill by alternating retrieves with both dogs.

By now, if you followed the instruction in the first book, you're sending your dog on marked retrieves using his name. This becomes extremely valuable when we get to honoring, because your dog will very quickly understand that if he hears the other dog's name, he should stay put.

When you've drilled home the concept of honoring on land, it's time to move to water. As you probably found when steadying your dog over water, the dummy or bird splashing into the surf is a very big temptation to break. That is also true with honoring, so be prepared to correct your dog during the introduction phase.

Finish this drill by adding gunfire. The next step will be to add live birds.

Temptation Retrieve

You marvel at the nice, fat greenhead you just shot as it plummets headfirst into the pond. On command, your dog leaps from his platform, and in no time, he's on his way back with the duck's chestnut breast gleaming in the soft morning sun. Then you're startled by the unmistakable sound of whistling wings. You're standing up in the blind, completely exposed, but a pair of mallards descends anyhow. You pop the drake, which falls 30 yards beyond your dog. A dog with only basic skills might instinctively drop the duck in his mouth and go for the second bird. But an advanced retriever will complete the retrieve at hand and then take a line toward the second fall. Given the title of this book, let's see to it that your dog does the latter.

At the outset of this drill, it resembles the setup for the basic retrieve and early stages of force fetching outlined in my first book. Position your dog on a platform, and command him to hold a fetching stick. Your dog is force-fetched, so this should come easily. Then, toss a dummy out off to the side the dog. He knows better than to drop the fetching stick after being commanded to hold it, so correct him if he spits it out and try again. If he holds the fetching stick, remove it from his mouth and reward him by sending him to retrieve the dummy. This intro to the temptation retrieve should proceed fairly quickly.

When he's ready for the next stage, position two platforms five feet apart. Have the dog sit on one of them in front of you while holding a fetching stick, and position the second platform next to you on whatever side your dog heels. We are about to add a substantial distraction to the training, so at this point, you have the option of going back to the check cord as an added layer of control. Next, throw a dummy off to your side angled away from the platform beside you. For example, if the platform at your side is positioned to your left, toss the dummy off to your right and angled slightly in front of you toward the dog.

Then call the dog to the platform at your side. Be ready to correct the dog using the remote collar and/or check cord if he drops the fetching stick or veers toward the thrown dummy. Demand that he picks up the fetching stick and comes to you before he can fetch the dummy retrieve.

When he's come to the platform at your side holding the fetching stick, remove it from his mouth, and send him to fetch the dummy retrieve.

After the dog is successful several times, put him back on the platform in front of you holding the fetching stick. This time, however, call him to you, and when he's about halfway in, throw the dummy and keep calling the him to your side. If he goes for the dummy or drops the fetching stick, correct him with your remote collar and check cord. If he holds the fetching stick and comes to heel, send him for the dummy retrieve.

After he's accomplished this a few times, just extend the platforms to 10 yards apart, and repeat the drill, starting by calling the dog to your side, throwing a dummy, taking the fetching stick and sending him for the retrieve.

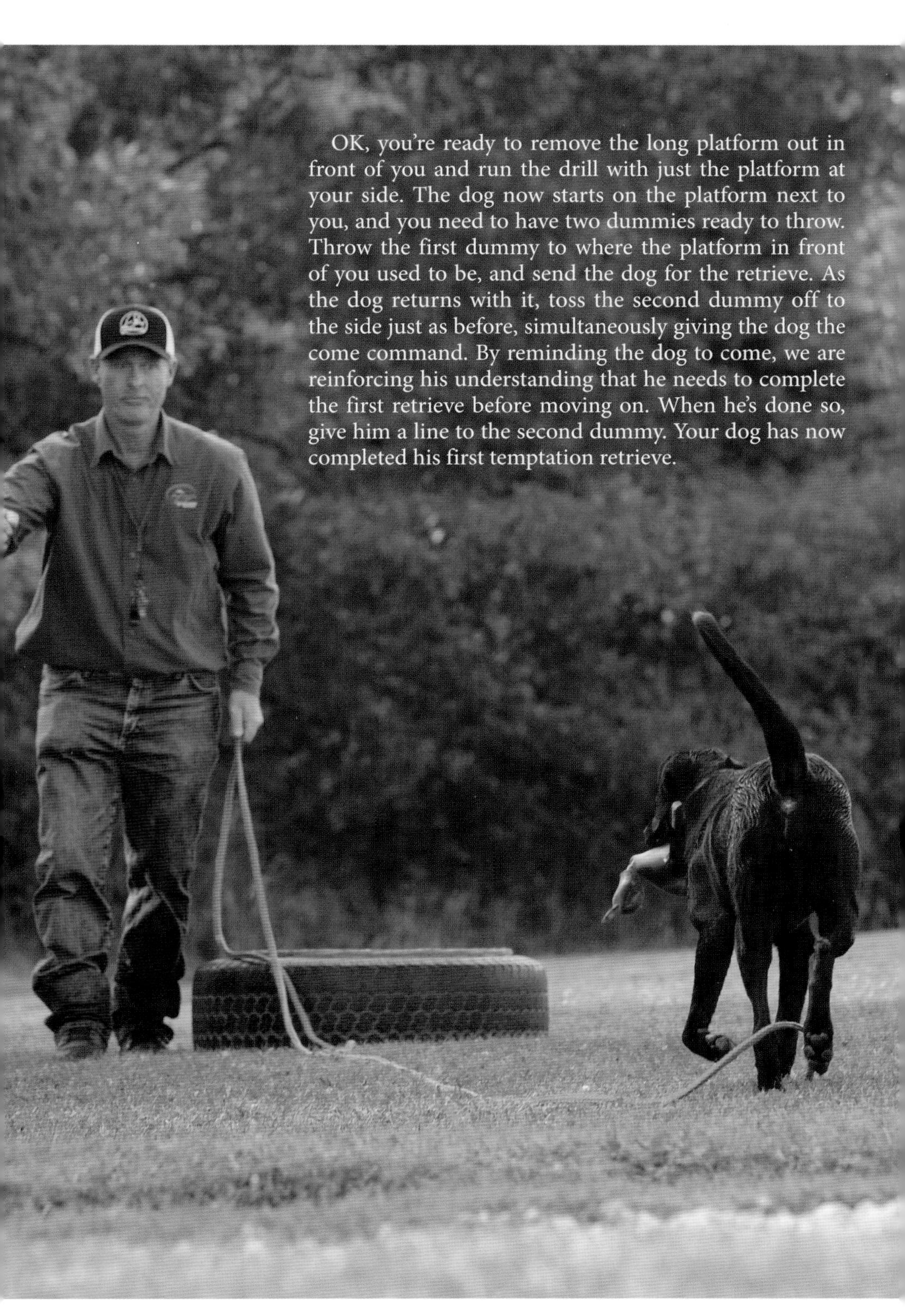

OK, you're ready to remove the long platform out in front of you and run the drill with just the platform at your side. The dog now starts on the platform next to you, and you need to have two dummies ready to throw. Throw the first dummy to where the platform in front of you used to be, and send the dog for the retrieve. As the dog returns with it, toss the second dummy off to the side just as before, simultaneously giving the dog the come command. By reminding the dog to come, we are reinforcing his understanding that he needs to complete the first retrieve before moving on. When he's done so, give him a line to the second dummy. Your dog has now completed his first temptation retrieve.

After he shows he's comfortable with it, we'll further tempt him to go for the second dummy by firing a blank pistol or shotgun as we toss it. This incites his adrenaline and encourages an error. Later we can add birds to the mix, which are even more desirable and tempting for the dog to veer off and grab. We need to tempt the dog as much as possible, because if training is easy for him, he'll never behave correctly in a hunting situation as circling birds, booming shotguns and ducks smacking the water raise his adrenaline to a fever pitch.

One last note regarding this drill: If you haven't noticed, your dog is now running a double retrieve.

Dummy Launcher

Especially if you train alone a lot, you must make sure you have the right equipment, and I absolutely put the dummy launcher in that category. Given that we're working with your dog on completing long retrieves, and this tool can

fire a dummy up to 100 yards over land or water, it is invaluable. Many people also don't realize how versatile it is. Did you know you can launch short retrieves with the launcher as well? Simply position the dummy toward the tip of the launcher, and it will go shorter. The closer the dummy is positioned toward the tip, the shorter the retrieve. And, just as with your shotgun, you can use heavy or light loads.

Diver Retrieving Dummy

In an ideal world, every duck you shoot would hit the water dead. But every waterfowl hunter knows that just isn't realistic, so no retriever's training is complete without teaching him to find cripples. This is particularly true for guys who hunt big water, as they're even more prone to the tragic experience of losing a bird. However, teaching your dog to hang with a crippled duck as it dives and resurfaces can be even more challenging than it sounds. Some dogs will swim halfway across a lake for a cripple, but others won't. Why? Often the dogs that give up were sent for a cripple early in their hunting careers, the duck dove and the dogs weren't able to come up with it. In turn, their confidence sank, the dogs lost interest in chasing down cripples, and they lost their usefulness as conservation tools. In the future, as soon as a duck dives, the dogs tend to remember their past failures, give up and come back in.

So, I've designed a tool called the Dokken Diver that builds my dogs' confidence early and ensures they'll chase down cripples in even the nastiest of conditions. It allows the

trainer to control the dog's first experience with a diving duck, because live crippled ducks can be very tough and unpredictable. Instinctively every time a bird dives, it will swim farther away, popping its head just barely out of the water as it makes a speedy, stealthy escape below the surface. If the duck isn't hit hard, it's almost impossible for an inexperienced dog to locate it no matter how many hand signals you give him. If you think your dog will learn to become a confident and proficient cripple chaser through trial and error on live birds, you're rolling the dice. This is even true in a training situation with a live, unshackled duck. Even in a small pond, the duck can elude a young dog.

This can be a real problem for all dog trainers, but with the dummy I use, you can simulate a diving duck. Best of all, you can control how long it stays underwater and when it will come to the surface — the one thing you can't control with a live duck. You can allow your dog to chase the dummy and pop it to the surface for the pup to grab at the opportune time to build the dog's confidence.

The dummy attaches to a heavy fishing rod and is cast into the water. On the first few retrieves, use the rod to pull the dummy underwater once or twice, just long enough for the dog to recognize the dummy dove and resurfaced. Nothing too challenging during this intro. As the dummy resurfaces in front of your dog, he'll grab it and confidently fetch it for you. Most will actually enjoy this new "game."

As the dog's confidence increases, keep the dummy underwater longer. When it resurfaces, allow the dog to swim toward it, and then pull it under again, and pull

it farther and farther from the dog before you pop it up again. You need to use good judgment in this scenario. Only increase the test if the dog is confidently pursuing the diving dummy. If at any point he seems unsure of himself, let him catch it to instill confidence. This is an invaluable tool for teaching any dog to stay with a cripple until it comes up for him to grab, and in my opinion, every duck hunter would greatly benefit from owning one. This can be used on young beginners as well.

Retrieving Geese

Many accomplished duck dogs fail on their first goose retrieve for the simple reason that they've never been asked to retrieve something so large. And unfortunately for young dogs, in most states these days, the first waterfowl season to open is for geese. Therefore, unlike in years past, the first wild-game retrieve many pups make is on a big Canada goose. You might have seen the result of this dilemma: The dog makes one feeble attempt to pick up the goose, but he just isn't sure how to do it and runs back to his handler. It has nothing to do with the dog's desire. He's just confused. Whatever you do, don't discipline the dog or go back to force fetching if this happens to you.

The dog simply must learn to adjust to larger-bodied fowl, which ideally occurs in a training situation rather than a trial-by-fire goose pit. Before your dog's first goose hunt, toss a similarly sized dummy for your dog so he can adjust and become accustomed to it. I'm a firm believer that if you don't train with something of the same size as the quarry you'll hunt, you're setting the dog up for problems.

Ensuring he's successful during the first goose hunt starts with training at home, but you also need to be cognizant of your decisions during the hunt. Hopefully, you don't shoot a 15-pound goose for the dog's first retrieve. Try to pick out a small one. And if he doesn't deliver it to hand initially, don't worry. Just toss the goose a few times for your dog before settling back in to hunt. He'll gain confidence and skill with every retrieve. Even if he just drags it a ways back at first, praise the effort.

Hunting Platforms

From boats, decoys, shotguns, blinds and assorted dog equipment, waterfowl hunters are gear junkies. And for good reason. Such gear allows us to hunt more effectively and, equally as important, more comfortably. The same goes for your retriever. Two items I consider required gear for his comfort are the hunting dog platform and neoprene retriever vest.

The platform is essential because you can't dictate where the birds will be, you need to go where they are. And in many cases, without a platform, your dog would need to stand in neck-deep water in order to hunt your particular honeyhole. That's just not going to work once the mercury starts to drop. Your dog should always wear a vest to help keep him warm, and stand on a platform to keep him dry and out of the water. He's not only more comfortable, but he'll also understand that the platform — which we've used throughout his training — is just an extension of the training environment. It reinforces that your dog should sit and wait until otherwise instructed. He's happier and much less likely to break or fail an honor. The same is true of strap-on platforms, which attach to trees in flooded-timber areas and are easier to use than regular platforms among submerged deadfall. Make sure to train with this piece of equipment before you go hunting.

After you can run your dog successfully on hand-thrown dummies, add helpers to throw marked retrieves as you run your dog from the platform.

—6—

MULTIPLE RETRIEVES

You don't necessarily have to teach every chapter in this book in chronological order. For example, it's your option to teach marked retrieves before blinds rather than how I've arranged them. However, in this case, Chapter 5's lesson on temptation retrieves flows nicely into our next drill, in which we'll teach the dog to make multiple retrieves. As your dog completed the advanced portion of the temptation retrieve, he was already technically making a double retrieve. The only difference is that rather than throwing two dummies right off the bat to start the drill, the second dummy was thrown in the midst of the first retrieve. Now all you need to do is build upon that.

Double Retrieves

For this drill, the dog will have to use his memory to complete a double retrieve. Before we rush in, let's get him feeling good about himself with an easy single. You will need a thrower, who should be positioned no more than 25 yards away in a large field of short grass. Have the thrower get the dog's attention verbally or by firing a blank gun as he throws the dummy. After the dog completes the retrieve, you're ready to introduce him to a double.

It begins the same way as the single: The thrower gets the dog's attention and throws a short retrieve. However, rather than sending the dog for the retrieve, turn so that you are facing angled away from it. Note that the dog should heel with you as you turn. Then, toss your dummy on this angle away from the thrower's dummy. If the dog heeled properly, he is facing the area of your dummy's fall and is ready to retrieve it. Send him on his name. If he goes for the thrower's dummy, call him back in, and send him for yours. However, the dog should be familiar with the concept of fetching the dummy he's facing, because we covered it during the wagon wheel drill.

As a general rule, the dog should always pick up the last bird that hit the ground first and then move on to the first bird that hit the ground. To successfully complete the double, he will need to remember where the thrower's dummy landed. That's why the first dummy thrown is known as the memory retrieve.

When the dog retrieves your dummy, turn and make sure you're lined up directly toward the memory retrieve. Give him a line, and send him. He shouldn't have too much difficulty finding the memory retrieve, given that this drill is similar to the temptation retrieve, the grass is short and the thrower is only 25 yards away.

After your dog grasps this basic intro to the double retrieve, it's time to add a second thrower to the equation. This person will toss the second retrieve rather than you. It's important in this initial stage that you keep the throwers spread widely apart so it's clear to the dog which dummy he's expected to retrieve. We must avoid tempting him to pick up the memory retrieve before he's done fetching the last dummy thrown.

To help the dog understand the next step in doubles training, Thrower A should get his attention and toss the memory retrieve to the exact same spot as before. Then Thrower B gets the dog's attention and, as he does so, you turn to face Thrower B so the dog does the same. Facing the retrieve tossed by Thrower B, send the dog on his name. Correct him with the e-collar if he goes for the memory retrieve instead. If the dog fetches the proper dummy, turn toward the memory retrieve, give him a line and send him.

As the dog's confidence increases, you can find a larger field of short grass and extend the lengths of both retrieves. Eventually, our goal for the memory retrieve is a distance of 250 yards, but it will take time to progress to that. As with lining drills,

back away from the thrower to increase the length of the memory retrieve, but the memory retrieve itself should always be thrown to the same spot. You know your dog by now. Be smart how quickly you incrementally increase the distance. However, any time we begin in a new field or extend the length of our double, it's important to start off with singles. Whichever thrower will toss the memory retrieve should toss a couple of singles for the dog to begin the drill. When you proceed to doubles, the memory retrieve should be tossed to that exact spot. This ensures that the dog will always have the confidence to run out for his more challenging memory retrieve. After one or two singles, simply add the second thrower and run the double as before.

At this stage, we are running what's known as a pattern double. We can run this drill in a half-dozen settings or so (and you should, so the dog knows the rules always apply regardless of his location), but essentially the throwers and retrieves are always in the same spot. The dog is essentially running the same retrieve multiple times and in multiple locations, and merely has to use his memory to be successful.

Triple Retrieves

The setup for a triple is very similar. Begin in an area where your dog has completed multiple pattern doubles with a high degree of confidence. After your throwers have tossed the memory retrieve and second retrieve, you will toss a third, very short retrieve off to the side away from the other two dummies. Communicating with your dog just as we did during the wagon wheel and double retrieve, have him fetch your dummy first, then the second dummy and then the long memory dummy. The dummy you tossed is an extremely easy retrieve, and after that, the dog is just running his old familiar pattern double again.

To clarify, you aren't testing the dog's ability to mark three retrieves concurrently right now. Because he knows the retrieve's pattern, you're basically just teaching him to count to three, and you're building his confidence in doing so. This will pay dividends when we get to the testing retrieve, in which the dog will have no idea where the throwers intend to toss the dummies. It's at that point he'll have to count the dummies and mark their falls. If at any time your dog struggles with the pattern triple, move the throwers back into 25 yards and try again.

If the dog is doing well, it's time to add another thrower to toss the third dummy rather than you. Remember to keep the throwers spread out to avoid confusion.

As the dog progresses on land — you guessed it — it's time to introduce double and triple pattern retrieves over water. Always start by running the memory retrieve as a single, and work into a double and eventually a triple. Start at a small pond, and move to larger ones to increase the distance.

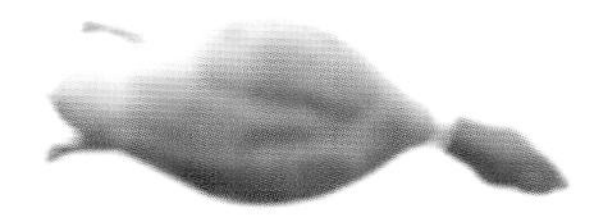

Multiple Retrieves from a Hunting Blind

For the dog to apply this training to a real-world hunting situation, he must practice it from whatever position he'll be in during the hunt. For example, will your dog hunt from a layout blind, dog stand, dog blind or other apparatus? As he advances in his pattern retrieves training, have your dog start the drill from the hunting equipment he'll use.

Another way to ensure this training best translates to actual hunting is to incorporate a shotgun. As the dummies are tossed, point your shotgun in the general direction of their falls. The shotgun should be unloaded, or you can fire blanks to add further realism and test the dog's steadiness. The dog will, in turn, begin to key on your shotgun and look in the direction it is pointed for his retrieves. This will help him in his training as we progress to testing retrieves, and it will have obvious benefits down the road when your gun is directed toward decoying waterfowl.

On that note, what if your dog breaks while your shotgun is up? You don't have a free hand to correct him, so I like to mount the transmitter for my remote collar directly onto my shotgun (see the photo on Page 220) within an easy thumb's reach.

Add a strip of Velcro to the forend of your gun and another to the back of your remote training transmitter to ensure it stays in place.

FRANCHI

–7–

ADVANCED UPLAND SKILLS

With a nose full of rooster scent, your retriever charges through the uplands while you follow in hot pursuit. The bird zigs and then zags, and for a moment, your dog loses its trail. He instinctively circles, relocates the scent and resumes the quest. Ten yards off the dog's nose, the pheasant flushes in an explosion of color and alarmed cackling. You mount your gun and quickly get off two shots, hitting the bird, but your pellets do not sufficiently crack its late-season armor. The rooster coasts down more than 100 yards away.

You send your dog, but your heart sinks. That was a long runner, and your dog worked darn hard to trail it. If only you could've come through. But the long-lines drill has paid off, and your dog takes an excellent path to the bird. Has it run? Your dog throws his head, indicating he smells the bird, and he confirms your fear by trailing it off to the right. You hold your breath as the dog goes out of sight. Twenty seconds later, a cackle breaks the silence, and you spot the bird, which momentarily reveals itself by hopping above the cover. You know your dog must be hot on it, and within an instant, he has it in his mouth — many dozens of yards from the spot the tough wild pheasant landed.

The feeling of watching a dog you trained perform thusly — versus the despair of losing a bird — is in itself enough incentive to instill advanced upland skills within him. There's arguably no greater benefit to having a good retriever in the field than when there's a wounded bird on the ground and it's running. I've seen retrievers trail crippled roosters a quarter-mile away from the hunters. There's just no way a guy on foot or, for that matter, a guy with a modestly trained dog could come up with such birds. So here's how to train to get the most out of your dog in the uplands.

Trailing Patterns

Before we begin, it's important that you have a piece of equipment that's required for any trailing drill: knee-high rubber boots. As any archery hunter knows, rubber boots do not leave nearly the scent as regular old leather. Therefore, by wearing them, you'll ensure your dog trails bird scent rather than your own.

Remember the basic straight line trail described in book No. 1? We're about to kick it up a notch. As you did for the basic drill, place a short rope on a dead bird, and drag it along the ground in a straight line, walking into the wind. Here's where it changes: After about 35 yards, make a gradual curve until you are dragging the bird at a 45-degree angle from the initial drag. Continue the drag in a straight line another 15 to 20 yards, and leave it there. Don't stretch this curved portion too far early on, because if it's too difficult for the dog, he might give up. That is definitely not a habit you want him to get into. Note: The flats in the accompanying photos

are used for illustration purposes only. The flags just show the curved trailing pattern. Do not use multiple flags when teaching this drill.

With the scent trail prepared, get your dog, put him at the start of the trail and command "hunt dead." Thanks to his prior training, your dog understands this command to mean that he's going to track a bird that has run. You'll repeat "hunt dead" as the dog works the line of the bird, simply to reinforce his understanding of it.

The dog should have little trouble with the straight-line portion of the trail, as this is old hat for him at this point. However, he might lose the trail as the curve begins. Give him time to come back and pick up the original trail, but don't overhandle — let him learn to work it out himself. You've kept the angle short, so he should find the bird eventually, even if you have to walk slowly toward it. Whatever you do, never allow your dog to fail. As always, he must find the bird or his confidence will suffer. When he sniffs out the trail, have him pick up the bird and fetch it to you, and then lay on the praise.

To best set your dog up for success, run this drill when scenting conditions are at their best to ensure the bird leaves as much scent as possible. In the morning with a light dew on the ground is ideal, and evenings are better than midday. If you don't have access to birds, I suggest using a dummy and adding a lot of scent to it, but a pigeon or other bird is always best.

After the dog is successfully and confidently taking an angled trail, you can start to get more creative with your drags. As long as the dog continues to progress, extend the lengths of your angles, make multiple angles and bends in your drags, and gradually work your dog out farther as you go. It's not unusual for dogs that trail wild pheasants to go extreme distances. I've seen dogs track down and flush birds 400 yards from the starting point, but we need to build gradually and work the dog out to that point.

Clip-Wing Duck Trailing

As a supplement to your bird drags, the use of a clip-wing duck, which cannot fly, can quickly boost your dog's bird-trailing abilities. Initially, run this exercise in a field of short grass that's no

more than a foot high. Release the duck, mark the spot where you let it go (an orange flag is perfect) and return in five to 10 minutes with your dog.

By then, the duck will have had a chance to waddle off a ways. Start the dog where you released the duck, command "hunt dead" and let him work out the scent trail. Given that you're using a live bird, and there's no possible way you've contaminated its trail with your own scent, this is a very realistic way to train for the real thing.

Remember, the longer you wait, the farther the bird is likely to go. Therefore, if you're starting with a beginner dog, don't wait an extreme length of time before you put him onto the scent. The bird could get away, or your dog might lose interest before it reaches the ducks. Either way, the dog's confidence is wounded.

You can also run this drill with a pheasant, but they tend to run much farther than ducks and could pose too great a challenge for your dog early on. In my opinion, you should avoid introducing pheasants until your dog can track a duck across a long distance. Alternatively, if you only have access to pheasants, you can tie the bird's legs together with a string, leaving a small gap. In this fashion, the bird's strides aren't as long and it will cover only slightly more ground than a duck.

Whistle Stop Tires

You and I are biased, so I reckon you'll agree that no gun dog is more capable of tracking a running pheasant than our retrievers. In fact, they're so good at it that sometimes we need to slow them down. Why? They can track a running pheasant faster than we can keep up. This can be a problem, because if you can't stop your dog, catch up and cast him back onto the bird's trail, guess what: The dog is going to flush the rooster out of range.

So, this drill will teach your dog to start and stop on command. This defies the dog's instincts when he's working scent, so we'll introduce the idea to him gradually. The first lesson begins with the placement of multiple training platforms in a straight line. Use a minimum of three platforms spaced no more than five yards apart.

Your dog starts the drill sitting on the first platform in the line, with you beside him. Command "place," and have the dog move to the next platform, just as we've done in previous drills. After he's atop the platform, use a single whistle blast to have him sit. Then walk ahead until you're beside the dog and command "place" so he proceeds to the third platform. Each time the dog reaches a new platform, use a whistle blast to have him sit, walk ahead to him and say "place" to send him to the next platform. Our goal is to teach the dog that when you reach him, you are ready for him to move up. Can you see how this relates to following a dog on a runner?

As the dog develops an understanding of this drill, we are going to repeat it, but instead of saying "place," we will use the command "place, go on." Eventually, we want your dog to advance to the next platform (or a running pheasant) on the command "go on," but at this point, we're simply introducing it. After your dog has run the drill for a few days using the new command, we will change it to "go on, place." If your dog advances to the next platform as soon as he hears "go on," don't bother saying "place." Just use "place" as a backup word in case you say "go on" and the dog doesn't budge. Soon, the dog will run the drill consistently with the command "go on."

However, if at any point the dog struggles, you can use a lead to guide him. This is unlikely, though, given that your dog has already undergone extensive platform training.

OK, time to advance the drill. The dog again sits on the first platform to start things off, but this time let the dog see you put a dead pigeon or other bird 15 to 20 yards past the last platform. He then has motivation to continue ahead of you rather than waiting, just as he will when he's actually tracking a running pheasant. Because we've introduced a new wrinkle to the drill, return for now to the place command so your expectations are crystal clear to the dog. After all, he's never been sent for a retrieve with the place command, so he'll understand he must go to the platform.

Advance the dog along the platforms as before, moving up, commanding "place" and hitting the sit whistle for each platform position. When the dog reaches the last platform, say his name to send him for the retrieve.

If all went according to plan, return your dog to the first platform, put a bird out (you can use multiple birds to up the temptation if you like) and run the drill again. The difference is that this time we'll use the command "place, go on" to advance him along the platforms.

Assuming your dog runs the drill without any issues, he's ready to return to the command "go on" or, if necessary, "go on, place" for the next run. Additionally, this time use the "go on" command rather than his name to send him for the retrieve. The reason for this is you are simulating the tracking of a running pheasant. You'd never say the dog's name in this scenario; you'd just have him continue on until he flushes the bird.

From there, you can move on to starting with the dog on a platform at your side and a bird out 40 to 50 yards in front of you, but without any platforms in between. This is tricky, because without any platforms to impede your dog, when you command "go on," he'll want to go straight to the bird. As he does so, let him go a few yards and use the whistle to stop him, but be prepared for him to disregard your command. After all, he thought he was getting the retrieve and was intent on doing so. So, have the check cord or e-collar ready to reinforce the command. When he sits, command "go on" and after a few yards stop him again. Then you can send him for the retrieve with his name.

As he progresses, you can eliminate the first platform, increase the number of times you stop the dog and use the command "go on" to send him for the retrieve. Your dog now knows the concept of stopping even though a bird awaits him.

The next step is to get your dog on a scent trail, which he already knows how to follow. Tell the dog to, "Hunt 'em up" and begin to follow along behind him. After a few yards, stop him with a whistle blast, reinforcing with the e-collar or check cord if necessary. After you catch up, command "go on" and resume following the dog as he trails the scent. Stop him several times along the trail, eventually allowing him to pick up the bird and retrieve it after one last "go on" command.

If your dog begins to stop on his own, especially if he does so often, it means you're stopping him too frequently. Just allow him to go greater distances before you stop him, and he should quickly shed this tendency.

Repetition, review and e-collar reinforcement of this drill will ensure your dog never flushes a running bird out of range. It's a really great skill and will no doubt put a smile on the faces of your hunting companions.

Quartering

A dog that will quarter the field in a nice, wide, back-and-forth pattern will always be more successful than one that courses the field in an irregular, random pattern. Quartering allows the dog to cover more ground, encounter more scent and flush more birds. Doing so is a natural instinct, but smart training helps bring it out, and you can extend the width of your dog's pattern by any degree you wish.

The easiest way to do so is with two helpers, one on either side of you as the three of you walk in a straight line down the field. Each helper should have a dead bird or at least a dummy. Have a helper on one side get the dog's attention, teasing the dog with the bird and continuing to do so as you cast your dog toward him. As the dog is running toward the helper, have him toss a short retrieve with his bird, and let the dog complete it. Then have the second helper repeat the process, teasing the dog toward himself and tossing a short retrieve.

At this point, the dog associates the helpers with retrieves and will look to them for more. However, this time we want the dog to quarter while we proceed down the field. Have Helper A tease the dog with his bird and cast the dog off. When the dog reaches the helper, have him quit teasing and hide the bird behind his back. At this point, you can introduce the dog to the concept of turning on the whistle by making two quick toots. As you do so, Helper B should immediately begin teasing the dog his way, shouting ,"Hey hey, hey!" and waving his bird. At this point, you and the helpers should also begin advancing down the field at a normal hunting pace. After the dog runs to Helper B, he quits teasing, you give your dog two quick whistle toots and Helper A calls the dog back to him. Continue teasing the dog back and forth in this manner as you proceed down the field. After the dog courses back and forth a few times, reward him by having one of the helpers toss a retrieve as the dog runs toward him.

You'll know when the dog's begun to understand this training scenario, because he'll start to turn on his own and require increasingly less teasing to quarter. At this point the helpers can carry live

pigeons with them as well as shotguns. As the dog courses back and forth, one of the helpers should dizzy a bird and roll it in while the dog's back is turned. Ideally the bird should be placed in just 12 inches of grass, and the dog should approach with the wind in his face. If the dog stops short of the bird, your helper should wave his hat or his hand and tease the dog over until he smells the pigeon. When the dog flushes it, the helpers can shoot the pigeon to reward the dog with a retrieve.

Alternatively, you can introduce your dog to flushing birds more slowly by having your helpers roll in clip-wing pigeons for him to find. Regardless, you'll soon find that your dog keys on the helpers and courses back and forth with great enthusiasm. Later your hunting buddies will be positioned in the same fashion, and the dog will quarter between them finding pheasants. To extend the distance that your dog will quarter, simply position your helpers farther out and repeat the drill.

Finish this drill by adding a working dog in front of the drivers. Demand that your dog is steady and honors the other dog's retrieves.

Posting

It's a common hunting strategy to position a few posters at the end of a field to block running pheasants while another group of hunters advances toward them. A poster actually ends up doing much more shooting than one might expect, but a poster's dog must sit patiently until the other hunters are done coursing the field. Few things are as frustrating as when a poster's dog takes off and wildly flushes birds out of range of the posters and well before the advancing hunters are nearby. Don't suffer this embarrassment.

It's very easy to train for a posting scenario. With the wind at your back, have a few helpers advance toward you, spread out in a

line across the field, just as they would be during a real hunt. Unbeknownst to the dog, you've hidden an electronic bird releaser in the field at least 15 to 20 yards away. As the helpers approach, release the bird, and have them shoot it. If your dog breaks on the retrieve or at any time moves from the sitting position during the drill, correct him with the remote collar.

During the helpers' next advance, you can release multiple birds during their approach. The dog must remain steady throughout the process, and each time a bird is shot, the dog should make the retrieve, come back and resume sitting patiently. Reinforce this with the remote collar if necessary, and in no time your dog will be ready to post.

–8–

RETRIEVER SAFETY TIPS

You just spent many months pouring your heart and soul into developing an advanced retriever. The reward ought to be the many years you'll spend enjoying a relationship with your dog and making fond hunting memories. However, too often, a dog's career is cut short, not because of age but because of an accident caused by his owner's negligence. Therefore, I've saved one of the most important topics of this book for last: retriever safety.

Keep an Eye on Your Dog

According to statistics, the biggest threat to your hunting dog's safety is an automobile accident. This does not need to be so. In fact, if every hunter would just abide by this rule, we could save countless dogs' lives: Your dog should always be the last thing

you take out of the vehicle before starting your hunt and the first thing you put away. Too often, as people arrive at their honeyholes, the first thing they do is let their dogs out. Next they gather their equipment, but meanwhile, their dog is scampering around along the edge of the road. Too often, such a scenario ends in tragedy.

Likewise you should always put your dog away before stowing your gear so he isn't running around in harm's way as you do so. I can't stress these tips enough. I've seen it happen too many times, and the results are never positive.

Skin Stapler

If you hunt upland birds, there's nearly always a barbed-wire fence somewhere nearby. Unfortunately, barbed wire is the No. 1 reason dogs get cut while hunting, and because a vet could be more than an hour or two away, you need to plan for such an emergency.

By far the best tool to stop the bleeding is a disposable skin stapler. A lot of people carry them, but many fail to practice before an emergency. How do they expect to use the stapler under duress if they've never familiarized themselves with it?

I've found the easiest way to do so is with a whole skin-on chicken from the grocery store. Simply make a slice in the skin, pull the skin flaps together and practice stapling them together. Soon you'll be prepared to use the stapler out in the field with your adrenaline pumping.

This is one piece of equipment that all hunters with dogs — but especially upland hunters — should carry.

Never Lay Your Gun Down

Failure to adhere to the next safety tip could prove fatal not only for your dog but to you or a hunting partner: Never lay a loaded shotgun on the ground or against an object such as a truck or fence. More than once, I've witnessed a dog running around haphazardly and knocking a gun to the ground. In an instant, you have a situa-

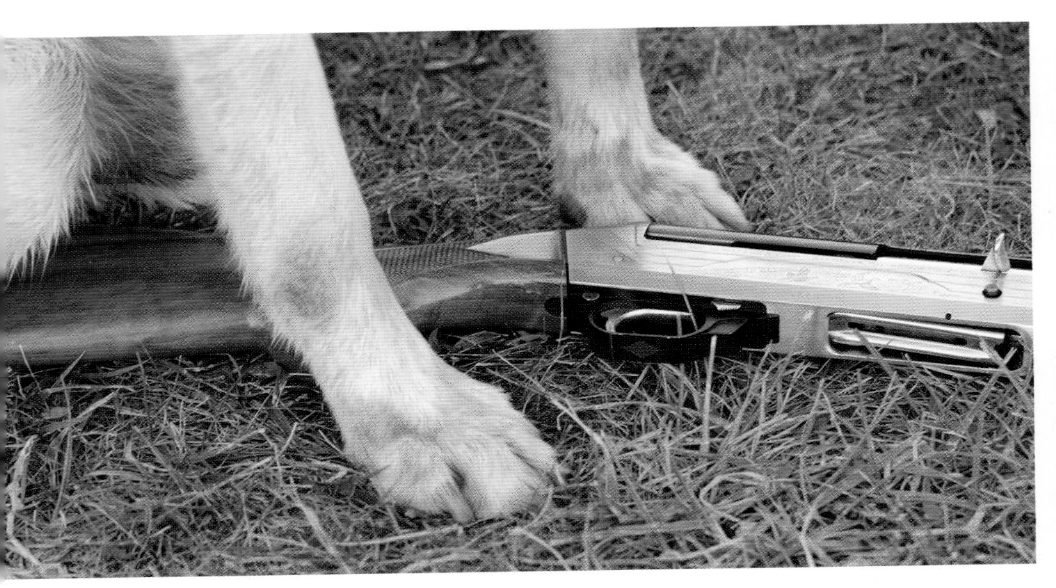

tion that's dangerous to everyone within gun range. A gun on the ground is only one dog paw away from simultaneously having its safety flipped off and its trigger squeezed. Make sure the gun is unloaded by visually and physically inspecting the chamber before you set it down. You can't account for what your dog will potentially do, but you can ensure you don't make this mistake.

Fences

We discussed the threat posed by barbed-wire fences earlier in this chapter, so it's important for your dog to understand how to go through them. As I approach a fence, I get my dog under control and lift the fence so the dog can make its way through. Note that it's always your job to be aware of your surroundings, including any terrain or structures that could create a bad situation for your dog. Barbed-wire fences are just one of the many potential dangers you could encounter in the field. So the bottom line is you must stay alert.

3BA129
DEC
CRITICAL HABITAT
12

Dog in Pickup Bed

Most people know better than to put an uncrated dog in a pickup bed, but it's amazing how much I still see this practice. This is infuriating, as it's not something to be chanced. You have a tremendous amount of time and emotion invested into your dog, so why jeopardize his life? A dog riding in the back of a pickup is just one minor car wreck away from death. There are even a few horror stories of dogs being leashed in the back of parked pickups only to jump over the side and hang themselves. Folks, when it comes to putting a dog in a pickup bed, just don't do it. The potential consequences far outweigh the convenience.

Cold Weather

As a waterfowl or upland hunter, I'm sure you're aware of the severely cold weather you might encounter afield. You need to protect your dog, and this includes travel to and from the hunt. So, if your dog will ride in a crate in the back of a pickup, a good, high-

quality insulated dog crate cover is a sound investment for such situations. Your dog might be wet from duck hunting or just too tired to efficiently warm himself, but a crate cover will give him the assistance he needs to withstand extreme cold. It acts as a barrier between him and the elements, and it's pretty amazing how much additional warmth such covers help dogs generate.

Additionally, many hunters put neoprene vests on their dogs to keep them warm, but very few use the vests when not in the actual act of hunting. Instead, have your dog wear the vest while traveling to and from the hunt for even more protection.

Frequent Inspection

Many times, cuts or lacerations that your dog suffers in the field — even mildly severe ones — aren't found until late in the day after the hunt's conclusion. Unfortunately, most veterinary offices are closed at that time, and if you're in an area without an emergency vet, you could be in real trouble. So during the day, especially at lunch, check your dog really well while he's resting and under control. Inspect his belly for lacerations, his eyes for seeds and other matter and his feet for debris, thorns and stickers. A little prevention goes a long way.

SOURCE YOUR OWN FOOD

Item #U2850 • Retail Price: $25.99

There's freedom in relying on the land rather than a store for your food. In *Recipes & Tips for Sustainable Living* you'll find creative ideas for food you source in your garden, in nature and on the hunt.

THIS GUIDE INCLUDES:

- Tips on gardening, food preservation and foraging
- Recipes for venison, wild turkey, duck, quail, small game and seafood
- Ideas for keeping bees and chickens

GROW YOUR OWN INDEPENDENCE

Buy Online at **ShopDeerHunting.com**
or call **1-855-842-5271** (weekdays, 8am–5pm CST)

U4689

GunDigest
WE KNOW GUNS SO YOU KNOW GUNS
THE MAGAZINE

ENTER TO WIN

NEW PRIZES BEING ADDED ALL THE TIME!

www.GunDigest.com

ENTER ONLINE TO WIN! CHECK BACK OFTEN!

NO PURCHASE NECESSARY TO ENTER OR WIN
Open only to legal residents of the United States and the District of Columbia age 18 years or older.
However, because of state regulations, this sweepstakes is not open to residents of Rhode Island.
All fi rearm transfers will be conducted in strict compliance with all applicable federal, state and local laws.
Limit: One online entry per person.